# LIVING WITH
# Yourself

## A WORKBOOK FOR STEPS 4–7

**Created by James Hubal and Joanne Hubal**

Based on material from *A Program for You: A Guide to the Big Book's* Design for Living* published by Hazelden Publishing

Hazelden
Publishing

---

*BIG BOOK is a registered trademark of Alcoholics Anonymous World Services, Inc.; used here with permission of AAWS.

Hazelden Publishing
Center City, MN 55012
hazelden.org/bookstore

ISBN: 978-1-5683-8990-5

*Editor's note:*

Hazelden Publishing offers a variety of information on addiction
and related areas. Our publications do not necessarily represent
the Hazelden Betty Ford Foundation's programs, nor do they
officially speak for any Twelve Step organization.

The Twelve Steps and Twelve Traditions are reprinted and adapted
with permission of Alcoholics Anonymous World Services, Inc.
Permission to reprint and adapt the Twelve Steps does not mean
that Alcoholics Anonymous has reviewed or approved the contents of
this publication, nor that AA agrees with the views expressed herein.
The views expressed herein are solely those of the authors. AA is
a program of recovery from alcoholism. Use of the Twelve Steps in
connection with programs and activities that are patterned after AA,
but which address other problems, does not imply otherwise.

This workbook has been updated to include both third-
and fourth-edition page references to *Alcoholics Anonymous*.

Cover and interior design/typesetting: Sara Streifel, *Think Creative Design*
Developmental editor: Marc Olson
Editorial project manager: Victoria Tirrel

# Contents

Introduction . . . . . . . . . . . . . . . . . . . . . . . . . . . . . . . . . . . . . . . . . .  1

**My Fourth Step** . . . . . . . . . . . . . . . . . . . . . . . . . . . . . . . . . .  3

Exercise 1   **What Is a Personal Inventory? Where Do Flaws
Come From?** . . . . . . . . . . . . . . . . . . . . . . . . . . . . . .  3

Exercise 2   **Roadblocks to Recovery** . . . . . . . . . . . . . . . . . . . . . .  5

Exercise 3   **Why Make a Moral Inventory?** . . . . . . . . . . . . . . . . .  6

Exercise 4   **My Resentments Inventory** . . . . . . . . . . . . . . . . . . .  7

Exercise 5   **My Fears Inventory** . . . . . . . . . . . . . . . . . . . . . . . .  16

Exercise 6   **My Sexual Harms Inventory** . . . . . . . . . . . . . . . . . .  24

Exercise 7   **My Miscellaneous (Other Harms) Inventory** . . . . . . . . .  31

Exercise 8   **Reviewing My Fourth Step** . . . . . . . . . . . . . . . . . . .  36

**My Fifth Step** . . . . . . . . . . . . . . . . . . . . . . . . . . . . . . . . . . .  39

Exercise 1   **Being Honest with Another Person** . . . . . . . . . . . . . .  39

Exercise 2   **Finding the Right Person** . . . . . . . . . . . . . . . . . . . .  40

Exercise 3   **Positive Changes That Will Happen** . . . . . . . . . . . . . .  42

Exercise 4   **Building an Arch to Freedom** . . . . . . . . . . . . . . . . . .  43

**My Sixth and Seventh Steps** . . . . . . . . . . . . . . . . . . . . . . .  45

Exercise 1   **Before Going Further** . . . . . . . . . . . . . . . . . . . . . . .  45

Exercise 2   **Hanging On to Character Defects** . . . . . . . . . . . . . . .  47

Exercise 3   **Replacing Character Defects with
Character Strengths** . . . . . . . . . . . . . . . . . . . . . . . .  48

Exercise 4   **Working Step Seven—Asking** . . . . . . . . . . . . . . . . . .  49

Exercise 5   **Practicing New, Positive Character Traits** . . . . . . . . . . .  50

The Twelve Steps of Alcoholics Anonymous . . . . . . . . . . . . . . . . .  53

The Twelve Traditions of Alcoholics Anonymous . . . . . . . . . . . . . .  54

# Introduction

The book *Alcoholics Anonymous,* commonly known as the Big Book, is the basic text for the fellowship of Alcoholics Anonymous (AA). It was published in 1939 to show how the first one hundred or so AA members found recovery from alcoholism. The founders of AA were Bill W., a New York stockbroker, and Dr. Bob, an Akron, Ohio, physician. Bill W. wrote the Big Book with the help of Dr. Bob and the other early members. He wrote the first 164 pages in a specific order that has not been changed or reworded since 1939. He wrote these pages so that if other alcoholics read the suggestions for recovery and put them into practice in exactly the order Bill W. wrote them, they would find recovery too.

Since 1939 millions of alcoholics and, more recently, countless people suffering from other addictive behaviors have done just that—they have found recovery.

This program of recovery is not a philosophy or religion. It is a practical *design for living* that is summed up in the Twelve suggestions, or Steps, listed on pages 59–60 of the Big Book and on page 52 at the back of this workbook. If you aren't familiar with the Twelve Steps, you should read them through carefully now.

———

The first three Steps show us how we can build a working relationship with our Higher Power, or God *as we understand God.* Steps One, Two, and Three are covered in the Big Book from page xxiii [page xxv, 4th ed.] to the bottom of page 63. The next four Steps—Steps Four through Seven—show us how we can better know and live at peace with ourselves. Steps Four, Five, Six, and Seven are covered in the Big Book from the last two lines of page 63 through the end of the second paragraph on page 76. Finally, the last five Steps—Steps Eight through Twelve—give us a design for living meaningful lives with other people and for continuing a daily program of recovery the rest of our lives. The Big Book covers these Steps from the third paragraph on page 76 to the end of page 103.

This workbook addresses Steps Four through Seven and is the second of three workbooks covering all Twelve Steps. All three workbooks were written to help you study the Big Book and apply what it says. Much of the text in these workbooks is adapted from the book *A Program for You: A Guide to the Big Book's Design for Living,* written anonymously by two AA old-timers. You will benefit even more from these workbooks if you read that book.*

While *A Program for You* is an optional supplement to these workbooks, a copy of the Big Book, *Alcoholics Anonymous,* is not—it is essential. Everything you need to know to be on the road to recovery from alcoholism (or another addiction) is in the Big Book. Anything else, including these workbooks, can only help you see what is already in the Big Book as you apply its suggestions in your life.

———

The Big Book and the fellowship of Alcoholics Anonymous are both concerned only with recovery from addiction to the drug alcohol. Neither the Big Book nor the fellowship makes any claim for what the suggestions in the Big Book will do for people other than alcoholics. Therefore, when referring to the Big Book or the AA fellowship, we will use the terms "alcohol" and "alcoholics."

Since the Big Book was written, many successful Twelve Step groups for recovery from other addictions and addictive behaviors have been established—Al-Anon, Cocaine Anonymous, Narcotics Anonymous, Overeaters Anonymous, and so on. While these groups publish their own literature, their basic program for recovery is not essentially different from the one described in AA's Big Book. In this workbook, when referring to recovery in general, or to you, the reader, we will use a variety of terms and references to include those who are not addicted specifically or exclusively to alcohol.

———

*A Program For You: A Guide to the Big Book's Design for Living* is published by and available through Hazelden Publishing.

# My Fourth Step

By doing Step Three, you have just made a very important decision—one, in fact, that may have saved your life. You have decided to begin the process of turning your will and life over to a Higher Power. This is an important decision, but one that will do little for you if it isn't followed up with action.

The first part of taking this action happens in Step Four. Here is the Fourth Step in the AA Twelve Step program:

**"Made a searching and fearless moral inventory of ourselves."**

Exercise 1
**What Is a Personal Inventory? Where Do Flaws Come From?**

> Turn to chapter 5, page 64 in your Big Book; starting with line 8, read to the end of the chapter on page 71.

What is a personal moral inventory, and why do alcoholics and other addicts need to make one?

On page 64, lines 8–16, the Big Book compares taking a personal inventory to taking an inventory in a store. Use the words in the list below to fill in the blanks below.

- continues to drink
- flaws
- damaged, unsalable
- finding, facing
- go broke
- searching, fearless

**A business inventory is . . .**

1. fact-_____ and
   fact-_____.

2. a search for _____
   and _____
   goods in order to get rid
   of them.

3. necessary, or the business
   will _____.

4. always in writing.

**A personal inventory is . . .**

1. _____ and
   _____.

2. a search for _____
   in order to get rid of them.

3. necessary, or the alcoholic
   _____.

4. always in writing.

If you are in recovery, you *are* in business—the business of staying clean and sober. In order to do this, you need to make a frequent, truthful, written inventory of your life. When you find damaged and unsalable goods—which are your flaws—you must face them, even if it's painful, and get rid of them promptly, without regret.

The Big Book says that the flaws found in a personal inventory all come from one thing. On page 64 of the Big Book, beginning with line 18, find the word that is the root of the alcoholic's problem and write it in the blank.

"Being convinced that _____, manifested in various ways, was what had defeated us . . ."

Look at the drawing below. You are standing on the Road to Growth and Recovery. To turn back means futility and unhappiness. To go forward means growth, recovery, and a relationship with a Higher Power. But on the road there are large rocks, which make a roadblock.

You will find on pages 64 to 71 of the Big Book that *SELF* shows itself in three main ways: *resentments, fears,* and *sexual (and other) harm to others.* Write one of these on each rock in the roadblock.

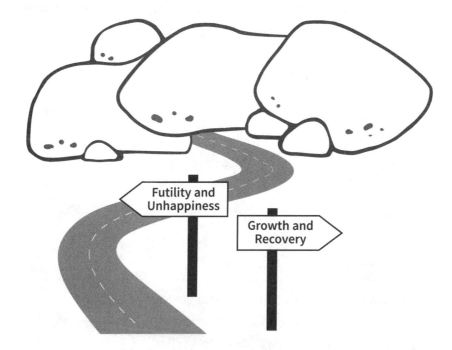

As long as you cling to your self-will, these three barriers will continue to block you off from a Higher Power. If you want to get rid of the roadblocks *SELF* puts up, you must be fully aware of them and their damaging effects on your life. Once your damaged thoughts—or flaws—have been removed, the barriers that block you from your Higher Power will also be removed. Instead of feeling restless, irritable, and discontented you can be clean and sober, peaceful, happy, and free.

The roadblocks on the Road to Growth and Recovery will be gone.

Duplicating this page is illegal. Do not copy this material without written permission from the publisher.

My Fourth Step    **5**

## Exercise 3
## Why Make a Moral Inventory?

In regard to our addiction to alcohol or other drugs, we know that we can't change the fact that we have a disease of the body, but we can do something about our illness of the mind. After reading, thinking, and talking about Step Four, you will begin to know that it is an action Step that will help you identify all the ways *SELF* blocks you from a Higher Power. If you don't do Step Four thoroughly, it is very likely you will eventually drink alcohol or use other drugs again.

Now answer in your own words: why do *you* need to make a searching and fearless written moral inventory of your life?

---

All in all, you will be asked to complete four inventories:
- Resentments Inventory
- Fears Inventory
- Sexual Harms Inventory
- Miscellaneous (Other Harms) Inventory

---

For now, we will focus on the Resentments Inventory. Like the other inventories, the Resentments Inventory will have an introduction, a set of directions, blank inventory forms for you to fill out, and a summary page. Use as many extra sheets of paper as you need to.

### Introduction

Resentment is a natural feeling. Everyone has felt it. In fact, sometimes resentment can be useful, like when it makes a person get up and act in a positive way. If all your neighbors paint their houses and clean up their yards, you might resent being left behind and get out and do the same.

What usually happens with alcoholics and addicts, however, is that resentment gets used in negative ways and makes things worse. When they get hurt by someone, they replay what happened over and over in their minds. If this goes on long enough, the resentment feeds on itself and they end up swimming in self-pity. Eventually, the resentment becomes the guiding force in their lives.

In the last paragraph on page 64, the Big Book calls resentment "the 'number one' offender" and says that resentment "destroys more alcoholics than anything else." When you're busy resenting somebody or something, that person or thing is at that moment controlling your life. Your resentment takes all of your time and energy, and doesn't leave any room for the guidance of a Higher Power.

All of this is why it's important that you start your personal inventory with a look at your resentments. If you can write down your resentments and look at them honestly, you'll be a lot closer to getting rid of them.

### Resentments Inventory Directions

> Take a look at the Resentments Inventory on page 12 in this workbook. You'll notice that it is divided into four columns, which we will now discuss.

Duplicating this page is illegal. Do not copy this material without written permission from the publisher.

My Fourth Step    7

### Column One (I'm resentful at:)

The way to take a personal moral inventory, using the Big Book's suggestions, is to do one column at a time. Do *not* go on to column two until the first column is done.

- Write down all the *people* you feel resentful toward, whether they're alive or dead. List them all, however few or many there might be.
- Then list any *institutions* you resent—the police department, the IRS, the post office, the church, whatever.
- Then list any *principles* (rules, ideas) you feel resentful toward—laws, moral codes, household rules, the Ten Commandments, Murphy's Law, and so on.

It might take you a while just to make a list of people and things you resent. You may end up with several pages of resentments. That's fine. What's important is that your list is thorough and complete.

If you have trouble getting started, just ask yourself who or what you're mad at. It will get easier as you begin writing.

> Go now to the Resentments Inventory on page 12 and fill in column one *(I'm resentful at:)*.

### Column Two (The Cause)

Once again, don't worry about filling in any of the other columns. Just go down column two from top to bottom, one item at a time. Look at each of your resentments; then, in a few words, write down its cause or causes, just as Bill W.'s imaginary alcoholic did on page 65 of the Big Book.

For example, if it's the police department you resent in column one, the causes in column two might be: "Arrested me for drunk driving when I only had a few," or "Took my license away, so I had to take the bus to work," or "Humiliated me in front of my family and neighbors."

If you're like most people, when you read what you've written in column two, you'll see that it's not the people or things that got you upset—it's what they *did*.

Look at the sample inventory on page 65 of the Big Book again. Bill W.'s imaginary alcoholic isn't mad at his wife because she's his wife—he's angry because she "misunderstands" him, "nags" him, and so on. If you look at the people, institutions, or principles on your list, you'll see that it is *what* they did to you that got you mad. Chances are you'd be just as upset if a different person, institution, or principle did exactly the same thing to you.

> Go now to the Resentments Inventory on page 12 and fill in column two (The *Cause)* from top to bottom, one item at a time.

## Column Three (Affects my:)

In column three write down which part or parts of you got hurt. Opposite each name in column one, list the area or areas of your life that were threatened or damaged by what this person, institution, or principle did.

People get angry when their instinctive needs for social belonging and acceptance (including self-esteem, pride, and nurturing relationships), security (both emotional and material), sexual relations (both hidden and acceptable), and plans for the future (ambitions) are threatened. In almost every case, we've found that one or more of these basic life issues that define our sense of *self* has been interfered with in some way. We can list these issues for use in completing column three *(Affects my:)* as:

1. Self-esteem

2. Pride

3. Personal relationships

4. Material security

5. Emotional security

6. Acceptable sexual relations (not hidden)

7. Hidden sexual relations

8. Ambitions

What we're calling acceptable sexual relations are those that won't harm you or someone else, and aren't in conflict with your values. Hidden sexual relations are those you feel the need to keep quiet from someone—your spouse or employer or parents or kids, for example. For a lot of married or partnered addicts and alcoholics, it means having sexual relations outside that primary relationship. For some of us, it's hiding a workplace relationship from our supervisor or other coworkers. While we wouldn't necessarily typify the hidden variety as a basic life issue, we understand that addiction has led many of us to engage in unhealthy sexual behaviors, and as such, they ought to be accounted for.

As you fill in column three from top to bottom, one item at a time, refer to the list of eight things that were interfered with. You may want to copy the eight items from the previous page onto another sheet of paper so that as you fill in column three, you can simply pick an item or items from the list and write them down.

For example, if it's the police department you resent in column one, and the cause of your resentment in column two is "humiliated me in front of my family and neighbors," in column three *(Affects my:)*, you might write, "Pride, personal relationships."

*A reminder: You can't give up your resentments unless you're first willing to admit and face them honestly. Pretending and avoiding the truth will only get in your way.*

 Go now to the Resentments Inventory on page 12 and fill in column three *(Affects my:)* from top to bottom, one item at a time.

### Column Four (S, D, F, I)

In column four you are going to look at each situation on your list that caused you resentment and then, forgetting about everyone and everything else involved, look at what *you* did to help cause the situation or make it worse. Were you **S**elfish, **D**ishonest, **F**earful, or **I**nconsiderate? This is the **S**, **D**, **F**, and **I** of column four.

It's easy to blame other people, institutions, or principles for everything. By doing that you can avoid looking at yourself or having to admit you weren't a total victim.

Once in a while, people do get hurt through no fault of their own. You may have been the victim of emotional, physical, or sexual abuse, for example. When you stop drinking alcohol or using other drugs, the tremendous feelings you have held back—the anger, fear, and shame—often rise up inside of you. If you've been abused in any of these ways, don't hesitate to seek qualified professional counseling to address your traumatic memories and experiences. This important work is beyond the scope of your Fourth and Fifth Steps but will be vital to your full recovery.

Usually, if you're honest, you'll see that most of the time you were at least partly to blame for what happened to you (though this is not the case with abuse). This means you play a role in your own resentments. After honestly looking at their inventories, some alcoholics and addicts discover that not one of their resentments is true. They had just transferred the blame to other people, institutions, and principles.

Now look at each one of your resentments in column one again. Except in cases of abuse (which are best processed with the help of a qualified professional), don't think about what other people, institutions, and principles did to you; instead, try to remember exactly what role *you* played in each situation.

Start with the first resentment on your list. Let's suppose it involves your boss. Look at what you've written in all three columns; then think about what you might have done to cause a problem for your boss so that he or she made trouble for you. Be searching, thorough, fearless, and honest about what you remember.

> As you look at each situation on your list and find out what your own part was in it, ask yourself what motivated you to do it. Were you Selfish, Dishonest, Fearful, or Inconsiderate? In the last column on your resentment inventory, write an **S** for selfish, **D** for dishonest, **F** for fearful, or **I** for inconsiderate. Sometimes you might write down two motivations, or even all four. Do this now on your Resentments Inventory.

# MY RESENTMENTS INVENTORY

| I'm Resentful at: | The Cause: | Affects My: | S, D, F, I |
|---|---|---|---|
|  |  |  |  |
|  |  |  |  |
|  |  |  |  |
|  |  |  |  |

# MY RESENTMENTS INVENTORY

| I'm Resentful at: | The Cause: | Affects My: | | | S, D, F, I |
|---|---|---|---|---|---|
| | | | | | |
| | | | | | |
| | | | | | |

*When finished, return to page 8 to learn how to complete column two.*

*When finished, return to page 9 to learn how to complete column three.*

*When finished, return to page 10 to learn how to complete column four.*

## Resentments Inventory Summary

> Now that you've finished your Resentments Inventory, look it over carefully from beginning to end.

Use what you've learned about yourself in your Resentments Inventory to respond to the following (use additional sheets of paper if needed):

1. You might see in column one that many of your grudges are against family members. You might realize that many of the causes of your anger in column two have to do with your job. You might see that self-esteem or hidden sexual relations seem to show up a lot in column three. Look at column four: have you been dishonest over and over, or selfish, or something else? *What patterns—things you do over and over—do you see in your inventory?*

Write what you've learned about your patterns. For example, "A lot of the time, I blame my spouse when I drink too much. This affects my personal relationships, but much of the trouble stems from my being dishonest about my alcohol use."

2. Once you know what it is you're doing or thinking over and over, you can work to make changes. Looking at the patterns you found in question 1, which ones will need the most work?

3. Another way this inventory will help you is by showing you where your anger and resentments are really coming from. Looking at what you wrote in column three, what part or parts of you are getting hurt most often? How will knowing this make it easier for you to get rid of your resentments?

4. In the past when you thought about the people and things that angered you, you probably thought about all the hurtful things they did to you. Right now, look at your inventory in a different way. Ask yourself what each of your resentments has done to you. How has it made you unhappy or closed you off from a Higher Power? How has it used up your time and energy? Worst of all, how have you used your resentments to continue your drinking or other drug use? *In other words, how have your resentments controlled you?*

Whether you feel your resentments are justified or unjustified, if you're clinging to them, they'll control your life. The fact is you need to let go of your resentments so that you can turn your will and life over to a Higher Power, and stop drinking alcohol and using other drugs.

5. What is it that the Big Book says you must do to get rid of your resentments? (See especially lines 14–24 on page 67.)

The Big Book tells you exactly how to make this happen. Read from the bottom of page 66, line 32, to line 13 on page 67. Doing what the Big Book says may seem strange or difficult at first, but the experiences of countless alcoholics and other addicts before you have shown that it is necessary to just *do it*. Do it once a day every day no matter what happens, and your resentment and anger will be gone.

Once you have rid yourself of your resentments, other things will begin to fill their place. Those other things are love, patience, tolerance, and goodwill toward your fellow human beings.

At this point, possibly the only thing keeping you from being free of your resentments is your fear of living without them. You're probably afraid of what life will be like with serenity, happiness, and peace of mind. Most of all, you're probably afraid of having to change.

In the next part of your personal inventory, you'll look at your fears and find out how to replace them with courage and hope.

Exercise 5
## My Fears Inventory

### Introduction

Most alcoholics and other addicts who are still drinking alcohol or using other drugs are deeply affected by fear. In fact, as the Big Book says on lines 27–30 of page 67, fear touches virtually every aspect of their lives.

This shouldn't be too surprising. After all, if you can't trust other people, if you won't trust a Higher Power, and if you can see your *SELF* starting to fail you, then you're going to be absolutely filled with fear. Sooner or later, you won't have anything or anyone to rely on, including yourself.

The Fears Inventory is a way of taking a close look at your fears in order to see how to get rid of them. Like resentments, you want to get rid of fears so a Higher Power can guide your thinking.

Some fear is good. It gives us the common sense to jump out of the way of a moving car or not eat poisonous mushrooms. But you need to get rid of the fear that shows up at the wrong place, at the wrong time and controls your life. The best way to do this is to do just what you did with your resentments: write down your fears, look at them carefully, understand what part you played in creating them, and see what your motivations were for doing that. In other words, make an inventory of your fears like the one you made for resentments.

**Fears Inventory Directions**

> Take a look at the Fears Inventory on page 20 of this workbook. It is divided into four columns. Get a pen or pencil and begin in column one. As you did before, you will be filling in the entire column before moving on to column two.

### *Column One* (I'm afraid of:)

List all the people, institutions, and principles that frighten you. List fears of all types—physical, mental, emotional, financial, whatever. Take the time to search these out and try to be as complete as possible. If you think of something later, go back and add it, or change your list.

Some of your fears might be about your job, your spouse, your children, the police, the IRS, and so on. They might be fears about what other people think of you or what other people might do to you. Some of your fears will make sense (we call these "rational" fears); some won't (these are "irrational"). You might have five or a hundred fears. Write them all down. Be complete and honest.

> Complete column one *(I'm afraid of:)* in the Fears Inventory on page 20.

## Column Two (The Cause)

Start at the top and go through each of the fears on your list, one by one. What caused it? Something the other person, institution, or principle did? Something you did? Something that happened to you years ago? Something that happened yesterday? Be simple and straightforward; don't psychoanalyze yourself. For each fear, write down the clearest, most direct cause you're aware of.

If you don't know and can't figure out the cause of a certain fear, write down "don't know" in column two.

> Fill in column two *(The Cause)* from top to bottom on the Fears Inventory, page 20 of this workbook.

## Column Three (Affects my:)

Here write down exactly what part or parts of you are affected by your fears—the parts of yourself you're afraid will get injured or destroyed.

Go through column three from top to bottom, one fear at a time, and list whatever area or areas of your life seem to be threatened in each case. Again, you might want to copy the list below of eight areas onto a piece of paper to use as a guide. Most of the time you'll be able to pick a word or words from this list to put in your inventory. If more than one area is affected by a fear, write them all down.

1. Self-esteem
2. Pride
3. Personal relationships
4. Material security
5. Emotional security
6. Acceptable sexual relations (not hidden)
7. Hidden sexual relations
8. Ambitions

> Go now to the Fears Inventory on page 20 and use this list to help you fill in column three *(Affects my:)* from top to bottom, one item at a time.

### Column Four (S, D, I:)

As you did with your resentments, go through your list once more, one fear at a time. This time, however, forget about what other people, institutions, or principles may have done to you to make you feel afraid. Instead, look at what *you* might have done to hurt or threaten each person, institution, or principle. What did you do that might have caused a problem for others so that they had to do something against you?

> For each situation write an **S** if you were **S**elfish, a **D** if you were **D**ishonest, or an **I** if you were **I**nconsiderate. If more than one letter is needed to describe your part in the problem, write all of them. Do this now on your Fears Inventory.

# MY FEARS INVENTORY

| I'm Afraid of: | The Cause: | Affects My: | S, D, I |
|---|---|---|---|
| | | | |
| | | | |
| | | | |
| | | | |

# MY FEARS INVENTORY

| I'm Afraid of: | The Cause: | Affects My: | S, D, I |
|---|---|---|---|
|  |  |  |  |
|  |  |  |  |
|  |  |  |  |
|  |  |  |  |

*When finished, return to page 18 to learn how to complete column two.*

*When finished, return to page 18 to learn how to complete column three.*

*When finished, return to page 19 to learn how to complete column four.*

Duplicating this page is illegal. Do not copy this material without written permission from the publisher.

My Fourth Step    21

### Fears Inventory Summary

▶ Now that you've finished your Fears Inventory, take a closer look at it.

Use what you've just learned about your fears to answer the following questions:

1. Look in each column. Do the same people or places show up over and over? What are you doing again and again to cause the problem or make it worse? What part or parts of you seem threatened? Which letters show up most often in column four? *In other words, what patterns—things you do over and over— do you see in your inventory?*

   Write what you've learned about your patterns. (Use more paper if needed.)

2. Once you can see your patterns, you can use them to help you make changes. The more a problem area shows up in your inventory, the more you'll need to work on it. Look at what you wrote in response to question 1. What are some of the things about your fears you need to work on the most?

3. For many people, just writing down their fears makes the fears seem less threatening, even silly. Now that you see your fears written down, have they changed? Do they seem as huge, threatening, and powerful as they did before?

How have your fears changed?

4. Like resentments, fears take up lots of time and energy. Have you avoided seeing certain people, going certain places, or doing things because of your fears? Has fear blocked out your Higher Power? *In other words, how have you been controlled by your fears?*

Now that you've looked closely at your fears, you may have seen how many of them began with your own actions and your own personality. This means that if you can change your actions and your personality, you can get rid of the source of your fears.

> Read lines 3–27 on page 68, of the Big Book, which says quite a bit about fear. At the end of this passage, the Big Book tells you exactly what to do to get rid of your fears. It also says the results will start right away.

5. What does the Big Book tell you to do to get rid of your fears?

As your fears leave, you'll feel less restless, irritable, and discontented. You'll begin to feel serenity and peace of mind. Your life will begin to change from one of fear and resentment into a life of happiness.

Exercise 6

## My Sexual Harms Inventory

### Introduction

Another area of your life that can block you off from your Higher Power is sexual relations. This area also seems to be one of the fastest and easiest ways to harm another person. Unlike other animals, who seem to just mate without feelings, human beings can give sex a lot of thought and planning. Humans are also responsible for their sexual behavior and the choices they make around it.

The Big Book (page 69), comes right out and says that *everyone* has problems with sex. It also says that AA will not be the judge of anyone's sexual conduct. The Big Book doesn't draw any sexual lines or tell you what you should or shouldn't do.

---

What should be clear, however, is that sexual abuse is not to be excused in any way. If you have raped or forced sexual contact on anyone or been involved in incest or any other sexual behavior with children, you will need to take some special measures beyond your efforts in Steps Four and Five. Whatever you need to do, whether it involves legal or psychological counseling, you must do it to be free of this block to your sobriety.

---

What the Big Book does do is give you a way to look at your past sex life to see if you harmed other people. If you did, then the Big Book will help you develop a new sex life for the future—one that doesn't harm others, and one that you can live with without becoming restless, irritable, and discontented. It will be sex without shame, fear, guilt, or remorse. Your new sex life might be with someone you've been involved with for some time and even someone you might have hurt in the past. But through taking this inventory, it will have a different basis—a basis of honesty and caring.

**Sexual Harms Inventory Directions**

> Take a look at the Sexual Harms Inventory on page 24 of this workbook. Like the first two inventories, it is divided into four columns. But you'll notice that the column headings on this inventory are a little different. You have probably also noticed by now that taking an inventory is a matter not so much of finding out who has hurt you, but rather of becoming aware of the people you've hurt or threatened, and finding out why you harmed them. The column headings for this inventory take that fact into consideration.
>
> This, of course, does not include sexual abuse—any sexual behavior that was forced on you against your will, either as a child or as an adult. As with any abuse you may have suffered, it is important to feel your anger and not fault yourself. You may need to seek qualified professional counseling to work through traumas like these. Do what you must to rid yourself of this resentment so that the person who hurt you no longer controls your thoughts and actions. If other people are still directing you, your Higher Power can't.

*Column One* **(I've hurt or threatened:)**

In column one list all the people, institutions, and principles you've caused trouble for through your sexual behavior. As you did before, fill in this column completely before moving on to column two.

Remember that it's possible to hurt many different people in many different ways with sexual behavior. For example, if you're married and have kids and you spend evenings having sex with someone else, then you've created problems for all kinds of people: your spouse, your children, the person you're sleeping with, maybe that person's spouse or children, and, of course, yourself.

Also list people you've harmed or threatened with your sexual behavior, regardless of their age or whether or not you've had sex with them. Maybe it was someone you flirted with or said sexual things to. Maybe your behavior involved someone very young. Make your list honest and complete.

> Go now to the inventory on page 28 and fill in column one *(I've hurt or threatened:).*

### Column Two (What I Did)

Go down your list in column one, and in column two write down what you did to cause each person, institution, or principle pain or trouble. You may have hurt someone by having sex with him or her, or by having sex with someone else besides that person. Maybe you ignored your partner's desires, insisting that your partner have sex with you the way you wanted it and when you wanted it. Maybe you've withheld sex and were cold to someone as a form of punishment. Maybe you had an affair with your best friend's partner and betrayed both a friendship and a religious code you value. All these sorts of things should be listed in column two.

> Stop here and fill in column two *(What I Did)* on page 28 of this workbook.

### Column Three (The Cause)

This is the place to write what it is in you that caused you to do the things you listed in column two. Because this is a sexual inventory, the two sexual categories you have used before are not included in the list of causes. Pick from the six areas listed:

1. Self-esteem
2. Pride
3. Personal relationships
4. Material security
5. Emotional security
6. Ambitions

> You may want to copy this list onto a piece of paper to use as a guide as you fill in column three *(The Cause:)* from top to bottom, one item at a time.

Sometimes people think that the reason they hurt someone with their sexual behavior is because of their sex instinct. Notice that "sex instinct" isn't even on the list. The sex instinct isn't an excuse for sexual behavior that hurts others. To be sexually aroused and feel absolutely nothing else is almost impossible.

---

Some alcoholics and addicts discover that their drinking or drug use masked additional problems with sex—such as compulsive sex or repeated, ritualistic sexual behaviors that harmed themselves and others. If this fits you, you may need to seek special counseling to deal with this other disorder.

---

Generally, if you look at your own past honestly, you'll see you were looking for something more than sex. Maybe you were trying to feel proud or secure. There's nothing wrong with many of these feelings. The problem comes when your desire for these things causes you to hurt other people. So even though the instinct for sex may be involved, it is a desire related to one of the six life issues (listed on the previous page) that leads you to hurt another person.

## Column Four (S, D, F, I:)

As you did in the other inventories, go back and look at the things you did to hurt people with your sexual activities. Forget about everyone and everything else involved, and ask what made you do what you did.

> In column four put an **S** if you were **S**elfish, a **D** if you were **D**ishonest, an **F** if you were **F**earful, and an **I** if you were **I**nconsiderate. The first thing you should notice is that your sex drive is not the cause of your sexual problems. The causes are **S**elfishness, **D**ishonesty, **F**earfulness, and **I**nconsiderateness.

## MY SEXUAL HARMS INVENTORY

| I've Hurt or Threatened: | What I Did: | The Cause: | S, D, F, I |
|---|---|---|---|
| | | | |
| | | | |
| | | | |
| | | | |
| | | | |

# MY SEXUAL HARMS INVENTORY

| I've Hurt or Threatened: | What I Did: | The Cause: | S, D, F, I |
|---|---|---|---|
| | | | |
| | | | |
| | | | |
| | | | |

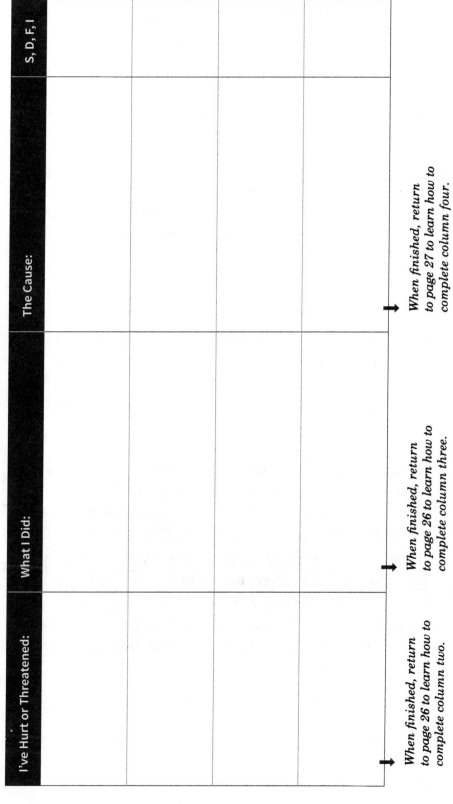

*When finished, return to page 26 to learn how to complete column two.*

*When finished, return to page 26 to learn how to complete column three.*

*When finished, return to page 27 to learn how to complete column four.*

### Sexual Harms Inventory Summary

Now that you've finished your Sexual Harms Inventory, take a closer look at it.

Using what you've learned in your Sexual Harms Inventory, answer the following questions:

1. What kinds of people are you hurting the most? Which sexual behavior is causing the most problems? *In other words, what patterns do you see in your inventory? Look in each column and write the things you see happening over and over.*

   Write what you've learned about your patterns. (Use more paper if needed.)

2. As you may have noticed before, the more often one of the causes turns up in column three, the more you want it. The more you want it, the more it controls you. It is important to know what you really want with your sexual behavior so you can work on the parts of it that are causing you to hurt yourself and others. For example, you may have had a series of affairs to boost your self-esteem or to get ahead in your career (ambition). If your sexual problems are not caused by your sex drive, what is it you really want? Use the information in column three of your inventory to help you decide.

3. As with resentment and fear, being sexually selfish, dishonest, fearful, and inconsiderate are personality defects that have control over you. These defects take a lot of your time and energy, and cut you off from your Higher Power. In what ways has your sexual behavior controlled you?

> The Big Book gives you a clear, practical set of suggestions for sexual behavior. These begin on line 25 of page 69 and continue to line 22 on page 70. Read them now.

4. In the space below, write what the Big Book tells you to do.

When you are wrapped up in a problem, you're also wrapped up in yourself. But when you work to help another person, you get so involved in what you're doing that you're automatically taken out of yourself. And once your *SELF* is forgotten, a Higher Power can take its place and start working in your life.

## Exercise 7
## My Miscellaneous (Other Harms) Inventory

### Introduction

By now you've done three personal inventories—one for your resentments, one for your fears, and one for your sexual conduct. In these inventories you've listed most of the people, institutions, and principles you've harmed or threatened in your life. But maybe there are still some that aren't listed on any of your three inventories. Maybe there are some people, institutions, or principles that you've caused trouble for in ways that have little or nothing to do with your fears, resentments, or sexual conduct.

To complete Step Four, you'll need to make a fourth and final inventory. You can call it a Miscellaneous (Other Harms) Inventory. Include in it any people, institutions, or principles you've harmed or threatened that you didn't include on your other inventories.

## Miscellaneous (Other Harms) Inventory Directions

> Take a look at the Miscellaneous (Other Harms) Inventory on page 34 of this workbook. It is divided into four columns.

### Column One (I've hurt or threatened:)

List all the people and things you caused problems for. Think of people, institutions, or principles that may not have been on your other lists. Perhaps you never actually hurt them but threatened to. For the purpose of this list, it's the same thing.

> Go to the inventory on page 34 and fill in column one *(I've hurt or threatened:)*.

### Column Two (What I Did)

In column two write down what you did to cause hurt in each situation or how you threatened someone or something. It could be something you did or said or threatened to do or say.

> Stop here and fill in column two *(What I did:)* on page 34 of this workbook.

### Column Three (The Cause)

As you've done with your previous inventory, write in column three the cause or causes for each of your behaviors that you listed in column two. Choose from the words and phrases below.

1. Self-esteem

2. Pride

3. Personal relationships

4. Material security

5. Emotional security

6. Acceptable sexual relations (not hidden)

7. Hidden sexual relations

8. Ambitions

> You may want to copy the "cause list" onto a piece of paper to use as a guide as you fill in column three *(The Cause)* from top to bottom, one item at a time.

### Column Four (S, D, F, I:)

> Go back and look over the behaviors you listed in column two. Decide what motivated your actions. Again, in column four put an **S** for **S**elfishness, a **D** for **D**ishonesty, an **F** for **F**earfulness, and an **I** for **I**nconsiderateness.

Duplicating this page is illegal. Do not copy this material without written permission from the publisher.

My Fourth Step    33

# MY MISCELLANEOUS (OTHER HARMS) INVENTORY

| I've Hurt or Threatened: | What I Did: | The Cause: | S, D, F, I |
|---|---|---|---|
| | | | |
| | | | |
| | | | |
| | | | |

*When finished, return to page 32 to learn how to complete column two.*

*When finished, return to page 33 to learn how to complete column three.*

*When finished, return to page 33 to learn how to complete column four.*

**Miscellaneous (Other Harms) Inventory Summary**

▶ Now that you've finished this inventory, take a closer look at it.

Using what you've learned from the Miscellaneous (Other Harms) Inventory, answer the following questions.

1. What patterns do you see in your inventory (people, places, types of behavior, causes of your behavior)?

   Write what you've learned about your patterns. (Use more paper if needed.)

2. Which of the eight life issues (as listed on page 33) are causing the most problems? Again, the ones that are causing you trouble are important to focus on, because they'll take work on your part to change. *In other words, which words and phrases are showing up most often in column three?*

   Is there anything else that you've learned about yourself by doing these inventories? If so, describe below.

---

You have now finished Step Four. You have completed a searching, fearless, honest, thorough moral inventory of yourself. Keep these pages to look back on in the future.

---

Use the questions below to review Step Four as described on pages 66 to 71 of the Big Book. Circle your choices. Cross out the options that are not included in the Big Book.

1. The alcoholic or addict needs to think of people who have wronged him or her as
   a. not worth helping
   b. just "bad apples"
   c. spiritually sick

2. The best way to get rid of bad feelings toward people is to
   a. wish the feelings away
   b. pray for tolerance
   c. stay away from people you don't like

3. It is important that the alcoholic or addict avoid
   a. retaliation or argument
   b. frightened people
   c. thinking about their flaws

4. The word that the Big Book says is "an evil and corroding thread" is
   a. fear
   b. drugs
   c. self-esteem

5. The remedy for problems from too much reliance on self
   a. making a list
   b. trusting in a Higher Power
   c. more confidence

6. Sex is a problem for

    a. alcoholics and addicts only

    b. men more than women

    c. everyone

7. Like other things, knowing what to do about sex problems will come

    a. from a Higher Power

    b. from good friends

    c. naturally with time

8. The goal of listing resentments and seeing all the problems they cause is to learn

    a. tolerance

    b. patience

    c. goodwill toward others

    d. all of these things

Doing the four inventories in an honest, thorough way was a big job. You should now have a clear picture of the way *SELF* has been a roadblock on your way to knowing a Higher Power and beginning recovery. You should also understand that it's absolutely essential that you continue to take action and to use what you've learned in your everyday life in order to keep moving toward growth and recovery.

The authors of the Big Book knew this and called chapter 6 "Into Action."

> The next Steps (Five, Six, and Seven) are described from page 72 to the end of the second paragraph on page 76 of the Big Book. Stop now and read these pages carefully.

Duplicating this page is illegal. Do not copy this material without written permission from the publisher.

My Fourth Step   37

# My Fifth Step

Here is the Fifth Step in the AA Twelve Step program:

**"Admitted to God, to ourselves, and to another human being the exact nature of our wrongs."**

## Exercise 1
## Being Honest with Another Person

Step Five has three parts. The alcoholic or other addict must admit their wrongs to

1. _____

2. _____

3. _____

After making your inventories, it shouldn't be too difficult to admit wrongdoings to yourself or to your Higher Power. But admitting these things to another person can be a very hard thing to do. According to the Big Book, pages 72–73, why is it important to tell your story to someone else? On the line below, write what the Big Book says is "the best reason." Then list the other reasons beneath the line.

_____

Duplicating this page is illegal. Do not copy this material without written permission from the publisher.

**39**

On page 73, starting on line 11, the Big Book says that more than other people, alcoholics lead a double life. Alcoholics, in fact, are actors. They want some people to see them one way (sober, responsible, etc.), while others see the drunken, out-of-control side. Because of this double life, it's especially hard for an alcoholic or addict to be totally honest with another person about those hidden parts.

> But Step Five says an alcoholic or addict must be totally honest with another person to overcome drinking or using other drugs. *This means your next job is to find the right person to tell your story to.*

Exercise 2
## Finding the Right Person

List every person you think might be a possibility for the job of listening to your story.

1. _____     6. _____

2. _____     7. _____

3. _____     8. _____

4. _____     9. _____

5. _____    10. _____

- Look over your list.
- Circle the names of the people you think are trustworthy.
- Put check marks by the names of the people you think would be willing and available to listen to you.

- Put stars by the names of the people who share or would understand, either by their own experience or on a professional level, your experience as an alcoholic or other addict.

- Now put a star by the name of each person who is familiar with the Twelve Steps of AA.

- Put a line through the name of anyone who would be hurt by or might judge you for anything you'd be saying.

By now it should be clear who would be the best person to talk to about your life story.

Write that person's name here: _____

> Do you still have any concerns about telling your story? If so, stop now and think of some ways to overcome your worries in order to make Step Five a success.

Now there is nothing left to do but to contact this person and set up a time to take Step Five—unless you have been unable to find someone you can trust right away and must postpone this temporarily (see the Big Book, page 74, lines 24–32 through page 75, line 2). You have found someone who will listen to your story. You have figured out how to get past your fears and worries about talking to this person. Now is the time to go ahead and do it. You may need more than one appointment, but you should reserve at least three or four hours to begin.

> On page 75, the Big Book gives exact directions on how to tell your story to another person. Read page 75, lines 3–12; then go and do it.

Many types of changes will occur after you tell your story to another person. Look over the items below and put a check mark by those found on page 75 of the Big Book. Cross out those that aren't found in the Big Book.

- You can look the world in the eye.
- You can get the job you always dreamed of.
- You can walk hand in hand with the Spirit of the Universe.
- You can be alone at perfect peace and ease.
- You can drink in a controlled way.
- You can forget about your Fourth Step inventory.
- You can begin to feel the nearness of the Creator.
- You can feel your fears fall away.

Look at the benefits you've checked. How do you feel about having these changes come into your life?

The Big Book says that by completing the first five Steps, you "are building an arch" through which you will walk as a free human being.

You are no longer alone. There is a helpful listener and a Higher Power. The rocks that made up the roadblock in your Fourth Step inventory have become the building blocks to a new way of living. You are therefore ready to continue the journey to growth and recovery.

On the building blocks of the new arch below, write a few words that sum up what the first five Steps have come to mean in your life. In the center of the arch write one sentence that describes what you will find as you move forward in your recovery.

# My Sixth and Seventh Steps

Exercise 1
**Before Going Further**

▶ Look again at the last paragraph on page 75 of the Big Book.

After you've taken Step Five, what does the Big Book tell you to do?

▶ Before you go ahead to Step Six, take some time to go back and review the character defects that you wrote about in your inventories.

Did you leave anything out of your inventories?  ☐ Yes  ☐ No

Were you honest?  ☐ Yes  ☐ No

Are your inventories thorough?  ☐ Yes  ☐ No

If you feel certain that you have not left anything out of your inventory, and if your answers to the two other questions above are *yes*, you are ready for Step Six—to let your Higher Power help you move forward. Here is the Sixth Step in the AA Twelve Step program:

**"Were entirely ready to have God remove
all these defects of character."**

On the mirror below, write your main defects of character, the ones that have caused you and other people the biggest problems. To help you with this, look back at your inventories and summary sheets to review your main character defects.

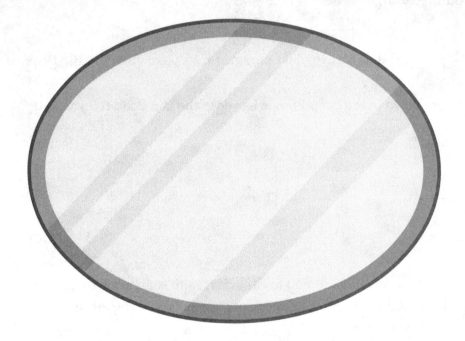

The words you've written on the mirror above are what you identified as your worst defects. Remember that Step Six says you must be *ready* to have God remove them.

- The Big Book (page 76) says that alcoholics don't always want to give up their defects. Sometimes it's easier to sit in today's pain than take a chance on something different. You know what your pain is like and you've learned to deal with it, but you don't know what the future will be like without that pain.

- Another reason it may be hard to give up defects is that some character defects are fun. They may cause other people trouble and lead to restlessness and discontent for alcoholics or addicts, but they're fun and you are unwilling to let go of them.

- Some people worry that if a Higher Power removes all their defects, they won't have any personality left at all. What really happens is that character strengths rush in to take their place. But some people don't understand or believe that this will happen, so some alcoholics and other addicts cling to the defects they've come to know.

Are you hanging on to any of your defects for the reasons just listed? Or for other reasons? If so, write about them here. (Use more paper if you need to.)

## Replacing Character Defects with Character Strengths

Let's take a closer look at one of the reasons why you might want to hang on to your character defects: you fear that you will end up with a "hole" in your personality.

This simply won't happen. Character defects will be replaced by character strengths. This means that where the defects used to be, you'll find *love, compassion, the will of a Higher Power, peace, serenity,* and *happiness.*

Write the words "I am filled with . . ." and then write each of these new character strengths.

Say these sentences out loud. How does it feel to state them as a part of who you are?

Practice thinking of yourself with these qualities and strengths.

When you understand fully that your character defects
will be replaced by character strengths, you're truly
ready to have a Higher Power remove all of your
old defects—and you will have taken Step Six.

From there it should not be hard to take the Seventh Step in the AA Twelve Step program:

**"Humbly asked Him\* to remove our shortcomings."**

First you were *ready* to ask, and now you *will* ask God, as you understand God, to remove your shortcomings. But how?

---

Exercise 4
## Working Step Seven—Asking

Read the Seventh Step prayer on page 76 (second paragraph) of the Big Book. Copy it in the following space, or write one of your own prayers, asking your Higher Power to remove all of your shortcomings. Asking God is the most important part, not how you say it. Write what seems right to you; then practice reading your prayer quietly to yourself.

---

\*Although the Big Book, written in the late 1930s, refers to "God" as "Him," no deliberate gender preference was intended. The word *Her* or simply *God,* depending on your preference, can be substituted for *Him.*

Once you've asked a Higher Power to take away your shortcomings, and once they've been replaced with new, positive traits, it's time to begin putting them into practice in your everyday life. This requires action and discipline. As with any new skill, these new ways of thinking and treating people take time to develop and become easier with practice.

These new, positive traits are honesty, unselfishness, consideration, and courage. Practicing these traits in your daily life means that, at first, you may have to make yourself do what you don't want to do and not do what you do want to do. This takes daily commitment and hard work. Slowly, the new, positive traits will seem more natural.

---

Exercise 5
## Practicing New, Positive Character Traits

Look at the chart on the following page. After each new character trait, write one situation from your life in which you will be called upon to practice this new skill, perhaps one in which it has been the most difficult to practice this skill in the past. For example, if you've been lying to your spouse for years about how you spend your paycheck, that might be the situation you'll write about in the space next to "Being honest" on the chart.

Under the New Way heading, write in a few words how you plan to handle each situation now that you've turned your old ways over to a Higher Power.

| New Character Trait | Situation | New Way |
|---|---|---|
| Being honest | | |
| Being unselfish | | |
| Being considerate | | |
| Being courageous | | |

As you practice honesty, unselfishness, consideration, and courage, something amazing will start to happen. The old you will disappear and die, and a new personality will take its place. You'll find this new personality and the new life that goes with it are far, far better than the life and personality you used to have.

As time goes on, and as you move on to the last five Steps, you'll see big changes in your life for the better. You will begin your journey on what the Big Book describes (page 75, lines 20–21) as "the Broad Highway, walking hand in hand with the Spirit of the Universe."

# The Twelve Steps of Alcoholics Anonymous[*]

1. We admitted we were powerless over alcohol—that our lives had become unmanageable.

2. Came to believe that a Power greater than ourselves could restore us to sanity.

3. Made a decision to turn our will and our lives over to the care of God *as we understood Him.*

4. Made a searching and fearless moral inventory of ourselves.

5. Admitted to God, to ourselves, and to another human being the exact nature of our wrongs.

6. Were entirely ready to have God remove all these defects of character.

7. Humbly asked Him to remove our shortcomings.

8. Made a list of all persons we had harmed, and became willing to make amends to them all.

9. Made direct amends to such people wherever possible, except when to do so would injure them or others.

10. Continued to take personal inventory and when we were wrong promptly admitted it.

11. Sought through prayer and meditation to improve our conscious contact with God *as we understood Him,* praying only for knowledge of His will for us and the power to carry that out.

12. Having had a spiritual awakening as the result of these steps, we tried to carry this message to alcoholics, and to practice these principles in all our affairs.

---

[*]The Twelve Steps of AA are taken from *Alcoholics Anonymous,* 3rd and 4th editions, published by A.A. World Services, Inc., New York, N.Y., 59–60. Reprinted with permission of A.A. World Services, Inc.

Duplicating this page is illegal. Do not copy this material without written permission from the publisher.

**53**

# The Twelve Traditions of Alcoholics Anonymous*

1.  Our common welfare should come first; personal recovery depends upon A.A. unity.

2.  For our group purpose there is but one ultimate authority—a loving God as He may express Himself in our group conscience. Our leaders are but trusted servants; they do not govern.

3.  The only requirement for A.A. membership is a desire to stop drinking.

4.  Each group should be autonomous except in matters affecting other groups or A.A. as a whole.

5.  Each group has but one primary purpose—to carry its message to the alcoholic who still suffers.

6.  An A.A. group ought never endorse, finance or lend the A.A. name to any related facility or outside enterprise, lest problems of money, property and prestige divert us from our primary purpose.

7.  Every A.A. group ought to be fully self-supporting, declining outside contributions.

8.  Alcoholics Anonymous should remain forever nonprofessional, but our service centers may employ special workers.

9.  A.A., as such, ought never be organized; but we may create service boards or committees directly responsible to those they serve.

10. Alcoholics Anonymous has no opinion on outside issues; hence the A.A. name ought never be drawn into public controversy.

11. Our public relations policy is based on attraction rather than promotion; we need always maintain personal anonymity at the level of press, radio, and films.

12. Anonymity is the spiritual foundation of all our Traditions, ever reminding us to place principles before personalities.

---

*The Twelve Traditions of AA are taken from *Alcoholics Anonymous,* 3rd ed., published by A.A. World Services, Inc., New York, NY, 564 [page 562, 4th ed.]. Reprinted with permission of A.A. World Services, Inc.

## About the Authors

Writers and educators James and Joanne Hubal bring to their work years of training and experience in various areas of expertise, including the field of addiction treatment. Joanne Hubal has been a writer, teacher, and cartoonist. She specializes in education and humor writing. James Hubal has developed and modified curriculum materials for schools throughout the country.

Since they were first published in 1991, the Hubals' *Living With...* workbooks, adapted from the material written in *A Program for You: A Guide to the Big Book's Design for Living,* have helped hundreds of thousands of recovering people engage and incorporate the Twelve Steps in their lives of healing and recovery.

———

## About Hazelden Publishing

As part of the Hazelden Betty Ford Foundation, Hazelden Publishing offers both cutting-edge educational resources and inspirational books. Our print and digital works help guide individuals in treatment and recovery, and their loved ones. Professionals who work to prevent and treat addiction also turn to Hazelden Publishing for evidence-based curricula; digital content solutions; and videos for use in schools, treatment and correctional programs, and community settings. We also offer training for implementation of our curricula.

Through published and digital works, Hazelden Publishing extends the reach of healing and hope to individuals, families, and communities affected by addiction and related issues.

For more information about Hazelden publications,
please call **800-328-9000**
or visit us online at **hazelden.org/bookstore**.

# Also in This Series

**A Program for You: A Guide to the Big Book's Design for Living**

This celebration of the basic text of Twelve Step recovery breathes new life into the Big Book's timeless wisdom. Thoroughly annotated, written with down-to-earth humor and simplicity, and providing a contemporary context for understanding, *A Program for You* helps us experience the same path of renewal that Bill W. and the first one hundred AA members did.

Item 5122 · 192 pages

**Living with Your Higher Power: A Workbook for Steps 1–3**

This workbook features information to reinforce important points in *A Program for You* and includes exercises for self-examination and disclosure. Clear discussions of Steps 1–3 and probing questions offer a guide to personal insight and reflection

Item 5421 · 52 pages

**Living with Others: A Workbook for Steps 8–12**

This workbook features information to reinforce important points in *A Program for You* and includes exercises for self-examination and disclosure. Clear discussions of Steps 8–12 and probing questions offer a guide to personal insight and reflection.

Item 5423 · 52 pages

# Other Titles That May Interest You

### A Gentle Path through the Twelve Steps
*By Patrick Carnes*

Renowned addiction expert and best-selling author Patrick Carnes, PhD, brings readers a personal portal to the wisdom of the Twelve Steps.

Item 2558 · 340 pages

### Twelve Step Pamphlet Collection

Used by patients in recovery centers throughout the nation, these easy-to-read editions are a sure way to gain a basic, and yet thorough, understanding of the significance of each Step.

Item 1455 · 12 Pamphlets

### Twenty-Four Hours a Day

A mainstay in recovery literature, "the little black book—*Twenty-Four Hours a Day*"—is the first and foremost meditation book for anyone practicing the Twelve Steps of AA. Millions of copies sold.

Item 1050 · 400 pages

## *Coming Soon*

### How We Heal

A diverse and inclusive meditation book for people with co-occurring sexual trauma and substance use disorders, this unique title brings together many individual voices to create a symphony of survivors all saying the same thing: you are not alone.